SPANI

LEARN 35 WORDS TO

Written by Peter and Helena Roberts

For the first-time visitor to Spain, Mexico, South America, or any other Spanish-speaking country

People may speak different dialects in different countries, but they will all understand well-spoken standard Spanish!

An English/Spanish language book, teaching you how to speak Spanish using 35 selected useful words.

First edition: January 2016
v1.1 : October 2017

Published in the United Kingdom
by
Russet Publishing
russetpublishing.com

Distributed internationally
by
Lulu Press Inc.
Morrisville, North Carolina, USA
lulu.com

Printed version
ISBN   978-1-910537-15-2

Also available as an electronic version

Comments and corrections welcome to
peter.roberts@russetpublishing.com

*"Learn 35 words to learn" is the copyright trade phrase
of Peter and Helena Roberts.*

A WORD FROM THE AUTHORS

This book was written by us after several visits to Spain. Before publishing, we have had it checked, and our initial errors corrected.

This piece of work, has been made by us for absolute beginners. We have received a good feedback from people visiting Spain for the first time, who used our 'Learn 35 words' system.

If you spot errors, please let us know. If you want to suggest corrections and improvements, or even just make general comments, please send them to us at:

peter.roberts@russetpublishing.com

Of course, if you have enjoyed our book, and if it helped you to enjoy your holiday, please also let us know. Many thanks.

Don't forget to learn the 35 words thoroughly *before* your holiday if you possibly can. On the other hand, perhaps it will wile away the time at the airport on your way out, or under a sun umbrella on a hot beach where you can then order your glass of water or lemonade fluently.

Wherever you read it, we are sure that, when you have studied it, it will make all the difference. And remember that a language book will mean more to you and will help you to remember vocabulary if you write notes in it and add your own words and phrases!

Best wishes from Peter and Helena Roberts.

Professional Input. *The core Spanish content of this booklet has been checked, corrected, and approved by a professional translation firm using a native-speaking Spanish translator.*

CONTENTS   5

INTRODUCTION

Learn 35 words. Speak Spanish

Yes, really! If you learn the 35 words that this book contains, you will be able to speak more Spanish than you ever thought possible in such a short time!

Try it and see. It will work!

Yes, it will take some time to learn 35 words, but it will be worth it the minute you arrive in Spain and start to speak in Spanish! We'll show you how!

This book was prepared by us to help you get around more easily. We know that within only one week, you will be able to ask for things in restaurants and in the market. You will ask directions, buy tickets, get on a train and arrive at the required destination, and have a good time.

That's why we printed this small booklet—so that anyone who wants to have a holiday in Spain, and who doesn't know any Spanish, can 'have a go'. With confidence!

Chapter 1 of the book contains the list of 35 words that you will need to know, together with a phonetic guide to their pronunciation. You will find it easy to learn them—make sure you learn them with the correct pronunciation.

Remember that **the pronunciation is very important**. Look at the phonetic part and practise each word faster and faster until it sounds like a single word. So that *dee-skool-pay* becomes *deeskoolpay*, which is, of course, di<u>scul</u>pe.

The emphasis is equally important. You will notice, that the emphasis is *often* on the next-to-the-last (penultimate) syllable of each word. On our list, there are six exceptions - *gr<u>a</u>cias, estaci<u>ón</u>, est<u>á</u>, fav<u>or</u>, mine<u>ral</u>, and ser<u>vi</u>cios.*

When you have learned the list and tested yourself thoroughly, you can move on to Chapters 2, 3, and 4, which will show you how to use the 35 words so that you will be understood for most of what you will need on a Spanish holiday.

Why only 35 words?

Because then you won't have to struggle with a phrase book when you want to speak! No waiter, bus conductor, or Spanish citizen is going to hang about while you struggle in a book to find the phrase you want, is he?

We hope that you have a wonderful visit to Spain, and that upon your return, our little booklet encourages you to have lessons and *really* learn how to speak the language. Good Luck.

Helena and Peter.

Chapter 1
Learn the 35 words.
Here's the magic list.

Unfortunately, there is no other way to learn this list but to sit down and study it for a few days. Our suggestion is that you set aside a regular time each day with someone else—preferably your proposed travel partner—and learn and test each other until you are absolutely sure that you know all of the words and can say their pronunciation correctly without thinking. Then you are ready to move on to Chapter 2.

The List

Don't forget that, in order to help you with the pronunciation, we have given a sort of amateur way of pronouncing each word, and we have underlined the part of the word that needs speaking strongly. i.e. emphasised. Practise until you can say each word quickly, and until you have remembered all of the words.

Note that the Spanish word may have an acute accent over a vowel. This means that this vowel is to be emphasised when it differs from the rule. It will match our phonetic underlining. For example: *están* pronounced *es-tan*.

1 **a**   un (m)   una (f)
   pronounced: oon   oo-na

2 **and**   y
   pronounced: ee

3 **are**   están
   pronounced: es-tan

4 **big**   grande
   pronounced: gran-day

5 **the bill**   la cuenta
   pronounced: la koo-en-ta

6 **a bottle**   una botella
   pronounced: oona bot-ay-ya

7 **cold**   frío
   pronounced: free-oh

8 **do you have...**   ¿tiene?
   pronounced: tee-en-ay

9 **entrance**   entrada
   pronounced: en-tra-da

10 **excuse me**   disculpe
   pronounced: dee-skool-pay

| 11 | **exit** | salida |
| | *pronounced:* | sal-ee-da |

| 12 | **free of charge** | gratis |
| | *pronounced:* | gra-tees |

| 13 | **a glass** | un vaso |
| | *pronounced:* | oon bas-oh (use a hard b) |

| 14 | **good evening** *or night* | buenas noches |
| | *pronounced:* | boo-ay-nas notch-es |

| 15 | **good morning** *or day* | buenos dias |
| | *pronounced:* | boo-ay-nos dee-as |

| 16 | **hot** | caliente |
| | *pronounced:* | kal-ee-ent-ay |

| 17 | **how much** (is it)? | ¿Cuánto (vale)? |
| | *pronounced:* | kwan-toe (ba-lay) |

| 18 | **is** | está   or   es |
| | *pronounced:* | es-ta   es |

| 19 | **no** | no |
| | *pronounced:* | no |

| 20 | **one** (1) | uno |
| | *pronounced:* | oo-no |

21	**please**	por fav**or**
	pronounced:	pour fab-**or** (a soft b)

22	**small**	*pe**que**ño.*
	pronounced:	pay-**ken**-yo

23	**station**	estaci**ó**n (feminine)
	pronounced:	es-tathy-**on**

24	**thank you**	**gra**cias
	pronounced:	**gra**-thee-as (use a soft th)

25	**that one**	**es**o
	pronounced:	**es**-oh

26	**the** (singular)	el (m)	la (f)
	pronounced:	ell	la

27	**this one**	**es**to
	pronounced:	**es**-toe

28	**ticket**	bi**llet**e
	pronounced:	bee-**yet**-ay (masculine, *un*)

29	**the toilets** (public)	los serv**i**cios
	pronounced:	loss ser-**bee**-thee-os

30	**train**	tren (masculine)
	pronounced:	train (as in English)

31 **two** (2)   dos
pronounced: doss

32 **I want (would like)**   Quiero (Quisi<u>e</u>ra)
pronounced: Kee-ay-row Kee-see-<u>ay</u>-ra

33 **water (bottled)**   agua miner<u>al</u>
pronounced: ag-wa mee-nay-<u>ral</u>

34 **where?**   ¿<u>don</u>de?
pronounced: <u>don</u>-day

35 **yes**   <u>sí</u>
pronounced: <u>see</u>

In Spanish, nouns are either masculine or feminine. This means that there are different words in Spanish for 'the' and different words for 'a'. In English we can just say 'the bottle' or 'a bottle', but not in Spanish.

At this "beginner's level" you won't have time to learn all the details so we suggest that you just try to follow the rule—getting it wrong some of the time. No one will mind.

For the masculine 'the' use 'el' (*ell*). e.g. e*l tren*
For the masculine 'a' use 'un' (*oon*). e.g *un tren*
El tren (the train), *un tren* (a train).

13

For the feminine 'the' use 'la' (*la*). e.g. *la estación.*
For the feminine 'a' use 'una' (*oona*). e.g. *una* estación.
La estación (the station), *una* estación (a station).

Also, to help with your pronunciation, the letter s is pronounced as in the English word *soft*. Not as in *cheese*.

The letter 'r' is pronounced strongly everywhere, including at the end of words—almost like an English d.

The letter v in Spanish is always pronounced as a 'soft b', except it is pronounced like the hard English letter 'b' when it is at the beginning of a word or after m or n. A hard b is pronounced as in the English word 'bat'. A soft b is pronounced as at the end of the English word 'tub', or even softer. Don't bring your lips together tightly— just touch them together gently for the perfect soft b.

The letter c before i or e is pronounced as a soft *th* as in the English words path or thick. Not as in that or brother.

- - - - - - - - oOo - - - - - - - -

So, have you really learned the magic 35 words? Or perhaps not!

If you have not, then go back to the list and keep learning until you can recall the words with no difficulty.

As we said before, learning the list is the hardest part of this job, but it won't take long if you really work at it. The morning time is the best time to learn things—when you are fresh. It's hard work in the evening when you're tired. So, find the first morning that you can—preferably before you go on holiday—and start to learn the list of 35 words. Then re-learn them the day after, and the day after and the day after. Five half hour sessions over five days will be much better than one two-and-a-half hour session. Of course, it's even possible to learn the words while you're on holiday. At least you'll have some time to do it.

If possible, ask a friend to test you, until you are perfect.

Normally, to speak Spanish, you will need about three years of hard effort and a private tutor. Most people don't want to put in that kind of effort or expense. For a first holiday to a foreign country, it's not necessary either. We know, because we've tried it.

On the other hand, it's murder on a holiday if you can't speak anything at all, and you feel stupid in a café, at a station, in the city, or when you want to buy something at a countryside stall or in a village shop. So, the following chapters show you how to put 35 words together to speak Spanish! It's true!

ADD YOUR OWN NOTES AND NEW WORDS HERE:

....

....

....

....

....

....

....

....

....

....

....

....

Chapter 2
I want something.
Don't we all?

Yes we all want something—mostly all of the time. We need a drink of water—especially in the summer in Spain.

We need to ask for lots of things like drinks, food, tickets in stations, the bill in a café, and so on.

OK. Believe it or not you already know how to do this!

I want….. It's a very useful statement, but it sounds a bit brusque in English, so we exchange it for the phrase 'I would like to have". That's better! But in Spanish, we only need to use one word—the rather more polite word *'Quisiera'*. You want something and it says it politely.

Quisiera. Yes—that's it.

What do you want? Lots of things, especially a drink of tea or coffee. You already know the word for tea—we didn't have to put it on our list. It's *tè* (pronounced tay).

I want tea please.
Quisiera tè, por favor.

That's it. Not very sophisticated, but it says it all doesn't it?
You can order some tea in a cafe already. And they will
understand what you want. You'll get some tea.

There is also coffee (*café*), pronounced ka-feh.
Black (They say 'a coffe only' ... *un café solo.*)
or white (They say 'with milk ... un café con leche.)
They don't say black coffee or white coffee as we do.

Quisiera un café solo.
I would like a black coffee.

And to top it off and make it sound even more polite, we add
the words for 'please' - *por favor.* (pronounced pour fab-or)

Quisiera un café solo, por favor.
I want a black coffee, please.

Quisiera un café con leche, por favor.
I would like a white coffee, please.

Quisiera un vaso de agua por favor.
(pronounced Kee-see-ay-ra oon ba-so day ag-wa por fab-or)
I want a glass of water please.

Esto es bueno.
This is good.

Quisiera una botella de agua mineral con gas por favor.
(con gas means with gas - sparkling*)*
I want a bottle of sparkling mineral water please.

If you don't want your water fizzy, that's easy too. You don't have to try to think up an equivalent phrase for the English words 'still water', you just say *"sin gas"*, which means 'without gas'. (Pronounced 'seen gass'.)

In fact, there's another useful tip for every situation. If you know one adjective, but don't know it's opposite word, just add the word 'no'. For example, you want to say that your water is warm, but you can only remember the word *'frío'*, meaning cold. You can complain: '*Esta agua no está fría*'. This water is not cold. Or 'This is not good': '*Esto no está bueno*'.

Quisiera una limonada, por favor.
I want a lemonade, please.

Quisiera la cuenta por favor.
I want the bill please - in the restaurant or bar. Perhaps you actually don't, but someone has to!

That's it—you are in control of the situation in the cafe. But don't forget 'please' - *por favor*, and 'thank you' - *gracias*.

ADD YOUR OWN NOTES AND NEW WORDS HERE:

Here is a word that you might like to know. There will be others that you will want to note here as well.

'o' is the Spanish word for 'or'.   *Esto o eso.* This or that.

....

....

....

....

....

....

....

....

....

....

....

Chapter 3
To find something.
We often need to find places.

We all need to find something—mostly all of the time.

We need to know where to get a train, or a taxi, or where to buy a paper or a stamp. We need to find the right train. We need to find a garage. We need to ask for lots of things.

Most commonly, in our experience, we need to find the ladies or gents toilets.

No problem. You already know how to do this from your list of 35 words. You did say you'd learned them didn't you?

Dónde está 'where is'   *or*   *Dónde están* 'where are'

It's pretty easy.

¿Dónde están los servicios, por favor? Where are the services, please? Which, politely, means where are the toilets? It's not worth learning the words for male and female because 99% of toilet doors in public places have a symbol of a man or a woman on them—standard all over the world. You'll see which door is right for you when you get there!

¿Dónde está la estación?
Where is the station?

¿Dónde está un taxi?
Where is a taxi?

¿Dónde está un banco?
Where is a bank?

¿Dónde está el Hotel Hilton?
Where is the Hilton hotel?

Of course, we can add 'please' to make it more polite.

¿Dónde está el Hotel Hilton, por favor?
Where is the Hilton hotel, please?

Anyone who speaks fluent Spanish will tell you that the above sentences are basic. But they will work! That's the main thing. You have the option of standing in the town square like a goldfish with your mouth opening and closing and nothing coming out, or you can say something that is grammatically ok and gets you what you want. It's an obvious choice!

ADD YOUR OWN NOTES AND NEW WORDS HERE:

....

....

....

....

....

....

....

....

....

....

....

....

ADD YOUR OWN NOTES AND NEW WORDS HERE:

....

....

....

....

....

....

....

....

....

....

....

....

Chapter 4
To buy something.
Don't we all want to do that?

Yes, we all want to buy something during our holidays—mostly all of the time. We need to buy presents, food, tickets, papers, postcards, etcetera.

So we could try to teach you a list of a hundred different things that you might want to buy. However, to save you the trouble most of the time, you can learn two words that will stand in for nearly everything: 'this', and 'that'.

Nonetheless, if you're smart, you'll buy a small, English/Spanish/English pocket dictionary from your local bookshop before you go abroad. Then you'll have a list of thousands of things that you can ask for.

Ultimately, of course, you can use your finger to point to something when you want it.

I want this! or I want that! It's easy in English—and in Spanish

You learned the words on the list so…

Quisiera *esto*. (I would like this)   or   Quisiera *eso, por favor.* (I would like that, please).

It's easy. Now you can ask for anything in the world that you can actually see at the time. I want to buy this or I want to buy that. Just point to it. What could be easier?

If you want to look up words, then that is also fine. For example, you might want to look up the word for a postcard, or a stamp, and then ask for them in the shop, because you might not be able to see a stamp to point to.

If you look up the word for stamp in a dictionary, you will find that it's called a '*sello*'. Because it ends in 'o' it is masculine and therefore is '*un sello*'. (Pronounced say-yo.)

So you walk up to the counter in the shop/post office and say: *Quisiera un sello, para el Reino Unido, por favor* (ray-ee-no oon-ee-dough) It is simple but they will understand you! "I would like a stamp for the United Kingdom". And don't forget to be polite with *"por favor"* (pour fab-or)

Before you buy something, you may wish to check how much it would cost. So you need the word 'Cu*ánto*' from the list of 35 words that you learned. Just use it with '*vale*' to make '¿Cu*ánto* vale?'. It means 'how much does it cost?'

Or to be a bit more adventurous, you could say: ¿Cu*ánto* vale *esto?* How much does this cost?

Or when you have bought something, you could say, *¿Cuánto vale eso? How much is that?*

Of course you don't know enough Spanish to understand the number they say back to you, which is a kind of problem, but we found that you can often see on the electronic till how much the thing is if you are buying it, or ask them to write it down by using hand signals if you haven't yet bought it. It works a treat. Everything is in Euros, so they write it down and you understand! That's fairly easy!

A bit of a tip: we suggest that you carry around a very small notepad and ball point pen with you, so that you can ask people to write things down for you—such as the price of goods before you purchase them.

ADD YOUR OWN NOTES AND NEW WORDS HERE:

....

....

....

....

....

....

....

....

....

....

....

....

Chapter 5
To speak Spanish.
Your dream.

You wanted to speak Spanish when you bought this book.

Well now you can. With just the 35 words we have taught you, you can speak an awful lot.

You won't believe it until you try, but you can get by for an entire holiday. And, if you have bought a small dictionary, you will learn another 35 words while you are away and you will be well on your way. You might even go to classes back home and improve more. Who knows?

Anyway, here are some of the things that you can now say that you never thought you would.

Quisiera un café descafeinado.   (des-caffay-<u>naa</u>do)
I want a decaffeinated coffee.

Quisiera té para dos.
I want tea for two.

¿Dónde está la estación, por favor?
Where is the station please?

¿Dónde está el tren para Madrid?
Where is the train to Madrid?

¿Cuánto vale esto? Esta carta? (kwan-toe ba-lay es-toe)
How much is this? This card?

Quisiera la cuenta por favor.
I want the bill please.

Quisiera un café y dos vasos de limonada, por favor.
I want a coffee and two glasses of lemonade, please.

Disculpe. ¿Donde está el Hotel Majestic, por favor?
Excuse me. Where is the Majestic hotel, please?

You get on a bus and ask the driver or passengers
'*¿Disculpe. Para Madrid?*' (Excuse me. For Madrid?)
Simple. They will either nod and mutter '*sì*' or say '*no*' and
point you in the right direction. We have done this and it
really works.

¿Dónde está un taxi, por favor?
Where is a taxi please?

Quisiera una cerveza, por favor.
I want a beer, please.

There is red wine (*vino tinto*), pronounced bee-no tin-toe,
or white wine (*vino blanco*), pronounced bee-no blank-oh.)

Quisiera un vaso de vino blanco, por favor.
I want a glass of white wine, please.

Quisiera una botella de vino blanco, por favor.
(oona bot-ay-ya day been-oh blank-oh, pour fab-or.)

Don't you think that this is great? You have learned 35 words (plus a few more—sneakily) and you are speaking Spanish on your holiday. Well done!

And there are plenty of pages throughout this booklet where you can add your own new words. Soon you'll know a lot more than 35!

We hope you are as pleased as we were when we wrote this little book for ourselves, on holiday in Spain.

Please remember that what you have learned here is very basic and is just a start. To speak Spanish well, you need to read proper textbooks and go to classes with a good teacher. Or even get private lessons. We hope we have given you the incentive to do so.

But if you don't study the language more deeply, you can always take our booklet with you when you go to Spain again!

With best wishes,
Peter and Helena Roberts.

Printed in Great
Britain
by Amazon